MW00803694

HANS ZIM...
COLLECTION

Contents

Produced by
Alfred Music
P.O. Box 10003
Van Nuys, CA 91410-0003
alfred.com

ISBN-10: 1-4706-1527-4
ISBN-13: 978-1-4706-1527-7

Cover Photo: © Zoe Zimmer

www.hanszimmer.com

ABOUT HANS ZIMMER

Hans Zimmer has scored more than 100 films, which have, combined, grossed over 22 billion dollars at the worldwide box office. He has been honored with an Academy Award®, two Golden Globes®, three Grammys®, an American Music Award, and a Tony® Award. In 2003, ASCAP presented him with the prestigious Henry Mancini award for Lifetime Achievement for his impressive and influential body of work. He also received his Star on the Hollywood Walk of Fame in December 2010. Some of his most recent works include Steve McQueen's *12 Years a Slave*, Ron Howard's *Rush*, Zack Snyder's *Man of Steel*, History Channel's miniseries *The Bible*; the Christopher Nolan-directed films *Inception*, *The Dark Knight* and *The Dark Knight Rises*; and Guy Ritchie's *Sherlock Holmes: A Game of Shadows*. Upcoming titles include *Son of God*, *The Amazing Spider-Man 2* and Christopher Nolan's *Interstellar*.

2014
Divergent (Executive Score Producer)
Winter's Tale (Composer)
Son of God (Composer)
The Amazing Spider-Man 2 (Composer)
G I R L (Additional Arrangements)

2013
Man of Steel (Composer)
Hansel & Gretel: Witch Hunters (Executive Score Producer)
The Bible (TV Series) (Composer)
Captain Phillips (Additional Music)
12 Years a Slave (Composer)
Beyond: Two Souls (VG) (Music Producer)
Rush (Composer)
Bullet to the Head (Music Producer)
The Lone Ranger (Composer)

2012
The Dark Knight Rises (Composer)
Madagascar 3: Europe's Most Wanted (Composer)
Aurora (Composer)
The 84th Academy Awards: Celebrate the Music (Composer)

2011
Skylanders: Spyro's Adventure (VG) (Composer: Main Theme)
The Best of Hans Zimmer (Composer)
Crysis 2 (VG) (Digital Volume 1) (Composer)
Sherlock Holmes: A Game of Shadows (Composer)
Rango (Composer)
Crysis 2 (VG) (Limited) (Composer)
Pirates of the Caribbean - On Stranger Tides (Composer)
Crysis 2: Be Fast! (VG) (Digital Volume 2) (Composer)
Thelma & Louise (Score) (Composer)
Kung Fu Panda 2 (Composer)
Crysis 2: Be the Weapon! (VG) (Digital Volume 3) (Composer)

2010
Inception (Composer)
The Pacific (TV Series) (Composer)
Tron Legacy (Music Consultant)
Megamind (Composer)
Call of Duty: Modern Warfare 2 (VG) (Composer: Main Theme)
Henri 4 (Executive Score Producer)

2009
Monsters VS Aliens (Executive Score Producer)
It's Complicated (Composer)
Angels & Demons (Composer)
Sherlock Holmes (Composer)
Transformers: Revenge of the Fallen (Additional Music)

2008
The Dark Knight (2 CD Special Edition) (Composer)
Vantage Point (Music Consultant)
Casi Divas (Composer)
Frost/Nixon (Composer)
Kung Fu Panda (Composer)
Running the Sahara (Music Producer)
Iron Man (Additional Music)
Babylon A.D. (Executive Score Producer)
The Dark Knight (Composer)
Madagascar: Escape 2 Africa (Composer)

2007
Pirates of the Caribbean: At World's End (Composer)
The Simpsons Movie (Composer)
Pirates of the Caribbean: Soundtrack Treasures Collection (Composer)
Film Music of Hans ZIMMER (Composer)
Bee Movie (Additional Music)
Pirates of the Caribbean: At World's End - Remixes (Composer)

2006
Over the Hedge (Executive Score Producer)
The Da Vinci Code (Composer)
Pirates of the Caribbean: Dead Man's Chest - Remixes (Composer)
Urmel Aus Dem Eis (aka Impy's Island) (Score Producer)
The Holiday (Composer)
The Prestige (Executive Score Producer)
Pirates of the Caribbean: Dead Man's Chest (Composer)
Pirates of the Caribbean 2: Dead Man's Chest (Japan Limited Edition) (Compo

2005
Der Kleine Eisbär 2: Die Geheimnisvolle Insel (Composer)
Blood+ (Volume 2) (Music Producer)
Good Morning America! (Composer)
The Island (Music Producer)
The British Years (Composer)
House of D (Executive Score Producer)
Madagascar (Composer)
Wallace & Gromit: The Curse of the Were-Rabbit (Executive Score Produc
Backdraft (Silver Screen Edition) (Composer)
Gladiator Special Anniversary Edition (Composer)
The Ring Two (Composer)
Blood+ (Volume 1) (Music Producer)
Batman Begins (Composer)
The British Years (Composer)

2004
Thunderbirds (Composer)
Lauras Stern (Composer)
Spanglish (Composer)
Shark Tale (Composer)
King Arthur (Composer)

2003

Pirates of the Caribbean: The Curse of the Black Pearl (Composer)
Something's Gotta Give (Composer)
The Last Samurai (Composer)
Tears of the Sun (Composer)
Matchstick Men (Composer)
The Lion King Special Edition (Composer)
Ti Adoro (Additional Music)
Johnny English (Song Writer)

2002

Spirit - Here I Am (Single CD) (Composer)
Spirit: Stallion of The Cimarron (Composer)

2001

Stanley Myers : The Deer Hunter And Other Themes (Additional Music)
The Wings of a Film (Composer)
The Pledge (Composer)
Pearl Harbor (Composer)
Hannibal (Composer)
Black Hawk Down (Composer)
Invincible (Executive Score Producer)
Riding in Cars with Boys (Composer)

2000

Grouchyfriendly (Additional Music)
Celtica (Management)
Mission: Impossible 2 (Composer)
More Music From Gladiator (Composer)
The Road To El Dorado (Composer)
Mission: Impossible 2 (Soundtrack) (Composer)
Gladiator (Composer)
An Everlasting Piece (Composer)

1999

Heart of Africa Vol. 1 (Composer)
Endurance (Music Producer)
Hans Zimmer Guitars Vol. 2 (Composer)

1998

The Thin Red Line (Composer)
Antz (Executive Score Producer)
The Prince of Egypt (Collector's Edition) (Composer)
Armageddon (Additional Music)
The Prince of Egypt (Composer)
Armageddon (Soundtrack) (Additional Music)
Symphony of Voices (Composer)

1997

The Lion King Original Broadway Cast Recording (Composer)
The Peacemaker (Composer)
The Borrowers (Score Producer)
Critic's Choice (Composer)
Face/Off (Executive Score Producer)
Smilla's Sense of Snow (Composer: Main Theme)
As Good as It Gets (Composer)

1996

The Rock (Composer)
White Squall (Additional Music)
Muppet Treasure Island (Composer)
Broken Arrow (Composer)
Broken Arrow (Limited) (Composer)
The Whole Wide World (Music Consultant)
The Fan (Composer)

1995

Nine Months (Composer)
Beyond Rangoon (Composer)
Something to Talk About (Composer)
Crimson Tide (Composer)
Rhythm of the Pride Lands (Composer)

1994

Africa: The Serengeti (Composer)
Hans Zimmer Guitars Vol. 1 (Composer)
Renaissance Man (Composer)
I'll Do Anything (Composer)
The Lion King (Composer)
Africa: The Serengeti (Composer)
Drop Zone (Composer)

1993

Batman: Mask of the Phantasm (Expanded Archival Collection) (Musician)
Younger & Younger (Composer)
Cool Runnings (Composer)
Calendar Girl (Composer)
True Romance (Composer)
Point of No Return (Composer)
Batman: Mask of the Phantasm (Musician)
The House of the Spirits (Composer)

1992

The Power of One (Composer)
Millennium: Tribal Wisdom and the Modern World (TV Series) (Composer: Main Theme)
Radio Flyer (Composer)
Toys single - The Closing of the Year (Composer)
Memoirs of an Invisible Man (Synth Programmer)
Toys (Composer)
A League of Their Own (Composer)

1991

Backdraft (Composer)
Thelma & Louise (Soundtrack) (Composer)
K2 (Composer)
White Fang (Composer)
Regarding Henry (Composer)

1990

Days of Thunder (Composer)
Green Card (Composer)
Pacific Heights (Composer)
Fools of Fortune (Composer)

1989

The World of BBC TV Themes (Composer)
Driving Miss Daisy (Composer)
Paperhouse (Composer)
Burning Secrets / The Fruit Machine / Diamond Skulls (Composer)
Black Rain (Composer)
Black Rain (Limited) (Composer)

1988

Rain Man (Soundtrack) (Composer)
A World Apart (Composer)
Rain Man (Score) (Composer)

1987

The Last Emperor (Music Producer)
Castaway (Composer)

1985

My Beautiful Laundrette (Composer)
Insignificance (Additional Music)
Histoire d'O - Chapitre 2 (Additional Music)
La Vita E Adesso (Synth Programmer)

1982

Figvres (Music Producer)

1981

Bulles (Synth Programmer)

1980

Cathode Mamma (Synth Programmer)
Ashes and Diamonds (Synth Programmer)
The Black Album (Song Producer)

160 BPM

(from the Motion Picture *Angels & Demons*)

Composed by
HANS ZIMMER

Moderately bright ♩ = 160

160 BPM - 9 - 1

160 BPM - 9 - 8

ALL OF THEM!

(from *King Arthur*)

Composed by
HANS ZIMMER

Slowly, expressively (♩ = 76)

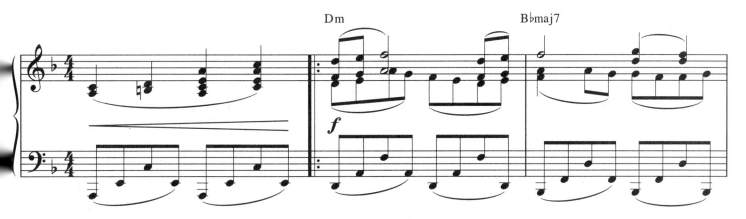

All of Them! - 7 - 1

Moderately (♩ = 86)

AH, PUTREFACTION

(from *Sherlock Holmes*)

Composed by
HANS ZIMMER

Moderately ($\quarternote = 80$)

Ah, Putrefaction - 2 - 1

(with pedal)

THE BURNING BUSH
(from *The Prince of Egypt*)

Composed by
HANS ZIMMER

Slowly, with expression (♩ = 60)

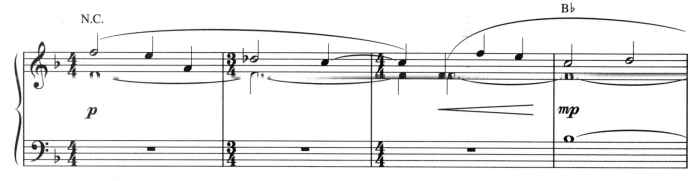

(with pedal)

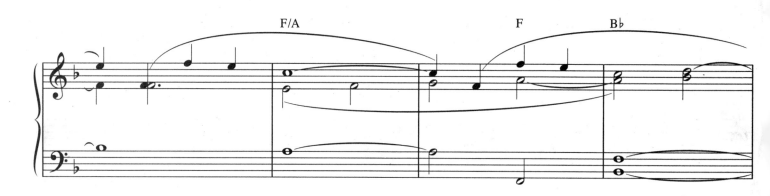

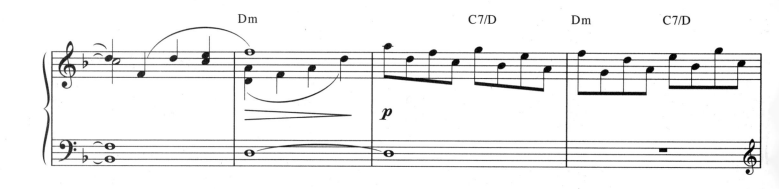

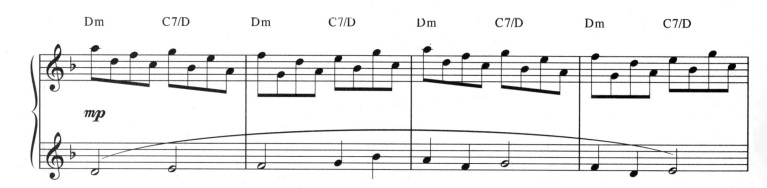

The Burning Bush - 2 - 1

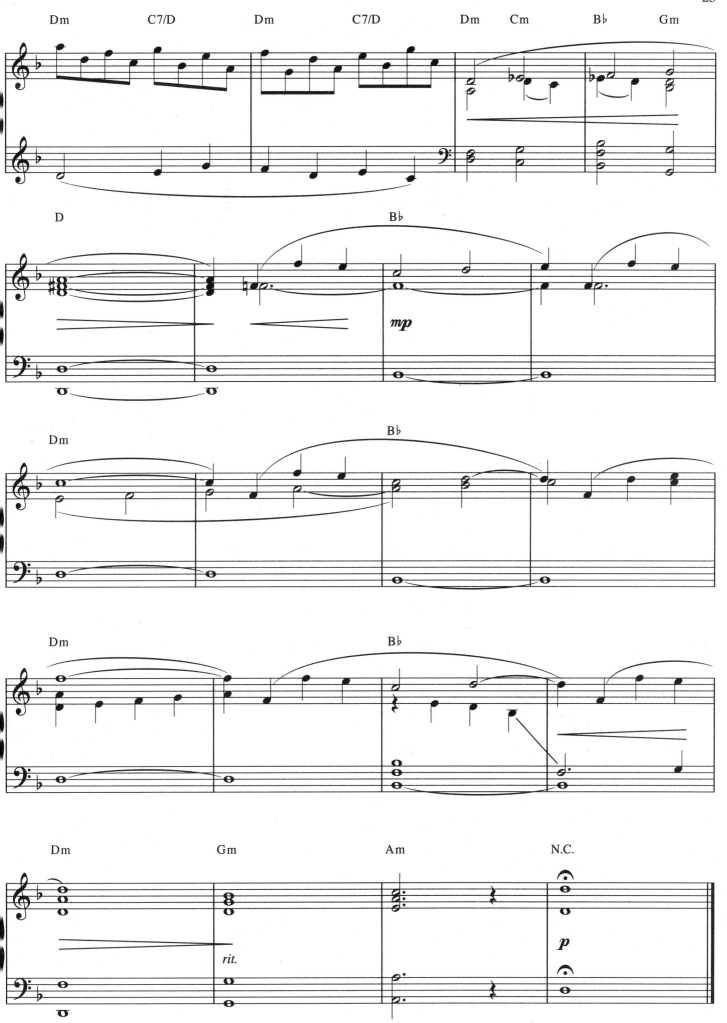

CAN YOU HEAR YOUR HEART?

(from *Winter's Tale*)

Music by
HANS ZIMMER, ANN MARIE CALHOUN
and RUPERT GREGSON WILLIAMS

Slowly and tenderly ($\quarternote$ = 73)

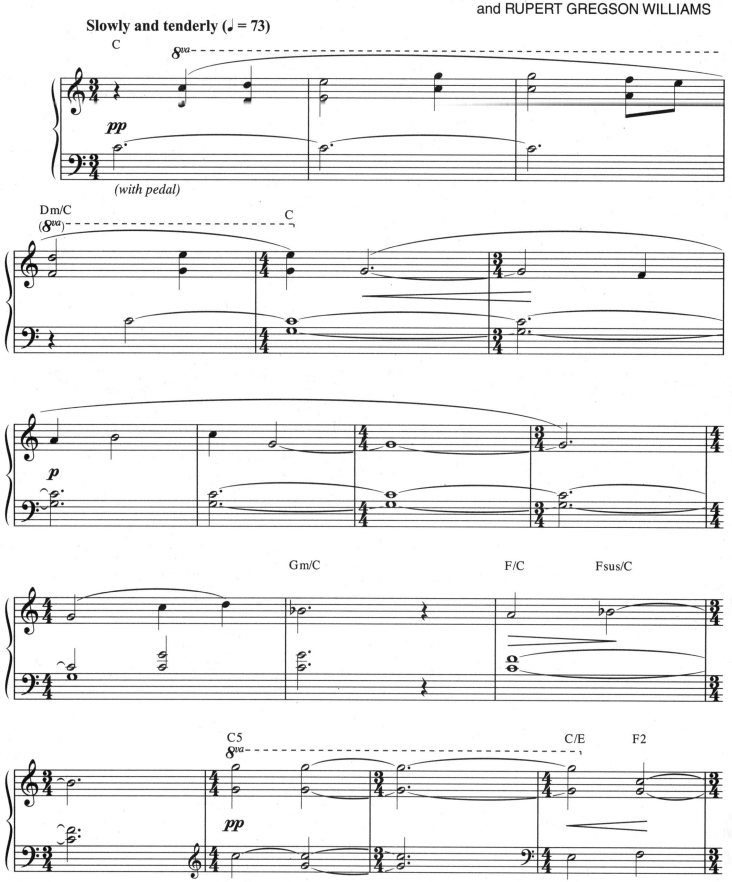

Can You Hear Your Heart? - 5 - 1

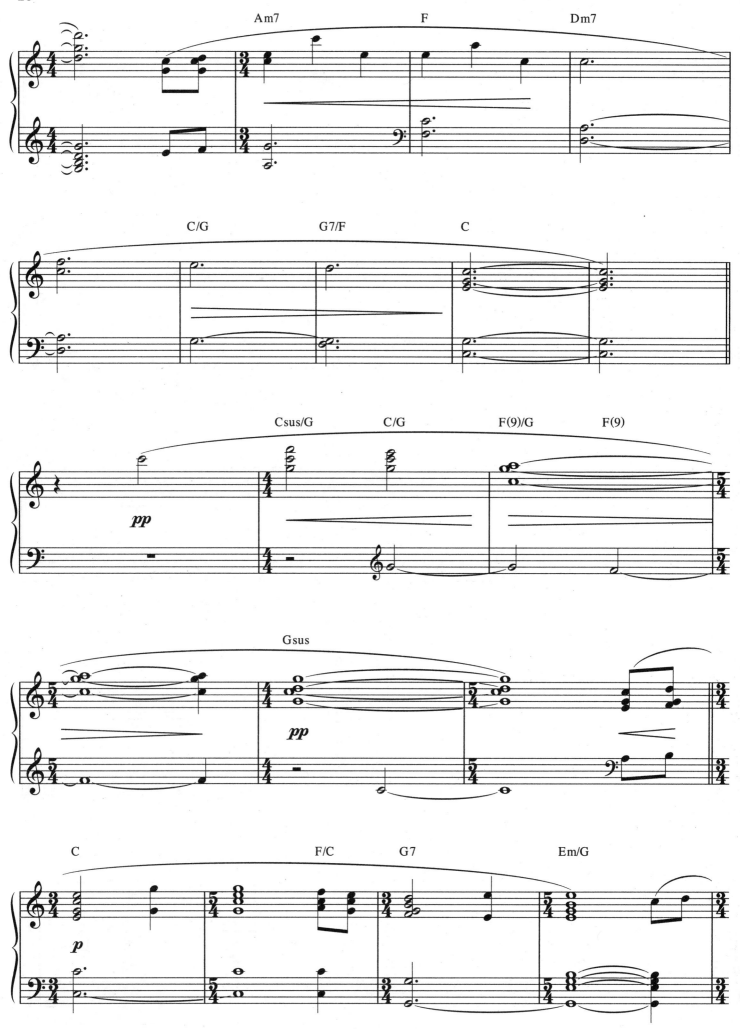

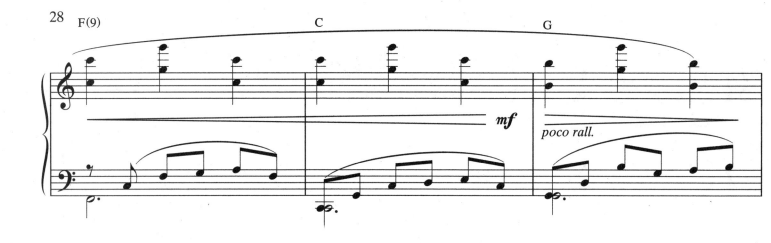

A little slower (♩ = 70)

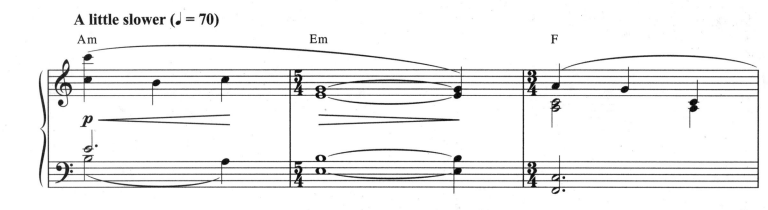

Slower (♩ = 60)

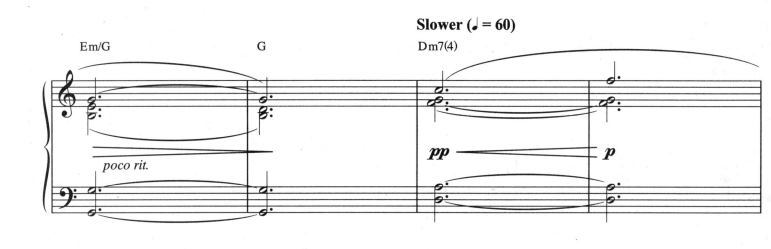

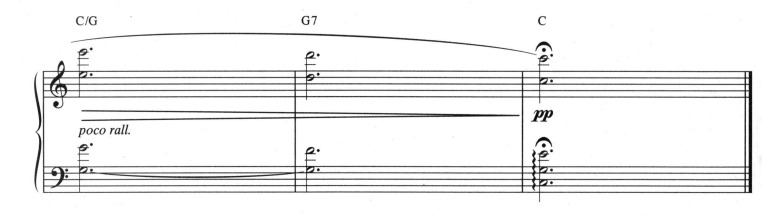

CORYNORHINUS
(from *Batman Begins*)

By
HANS ZIMMER,
JAMES NEWTON HOWARD, MELVYN WESSON,
RAMIN DJAWADI and LORNE BALFE

Moderately slow, rubato (♩ = 72)

Corynorhinus (Surveying the Ruins) - 3 - 1

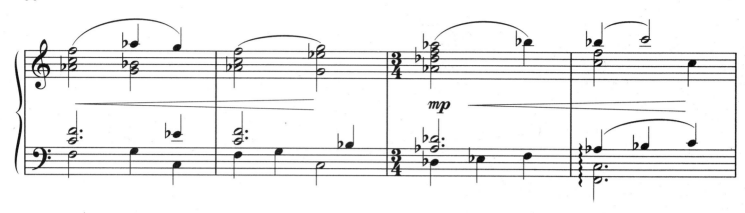

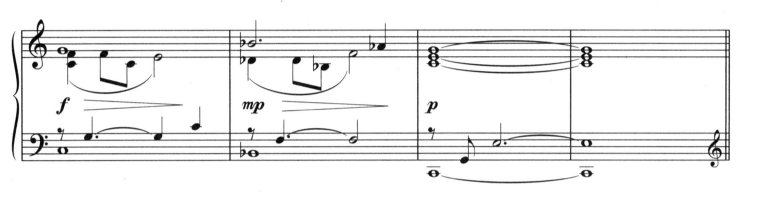

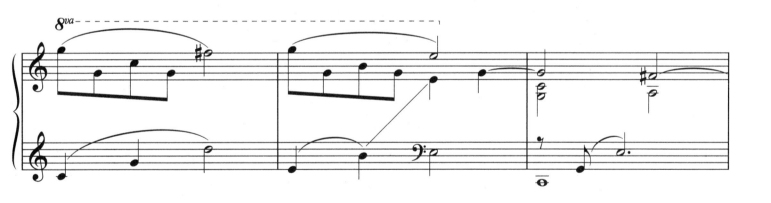

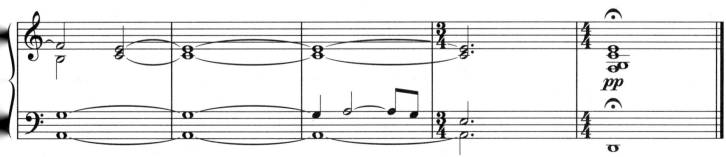

Corynorhinus (Surveying the Ruins) - 3 - 3

CHELDORADO

(from *The Road to El Dorado*)

Composed by
HANS ZIMMER

Moderate latin (♩ = 123)

(with pedal)

34

Moderately fast (♪ = 164)

...end solo)

Cheldorado - 6 - 6

CHEVALIERS de SANGREAL

(from *The Da Vinci Code*)

Composed by
HANS ZIMMER

Moderately (♩. = 56)

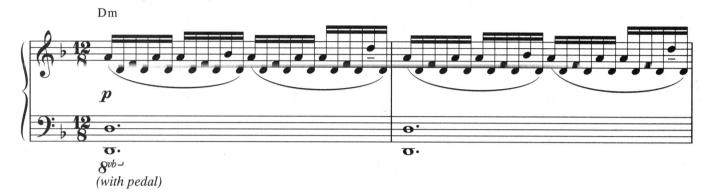

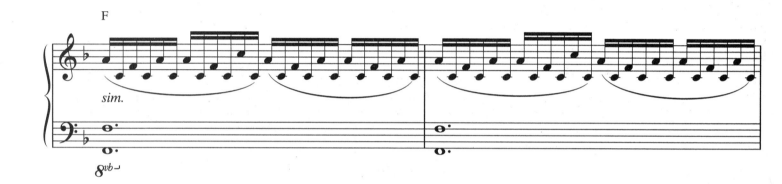

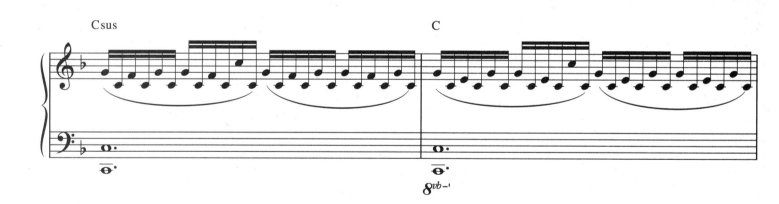

Chevaliers de Sangreal - 6 - 1

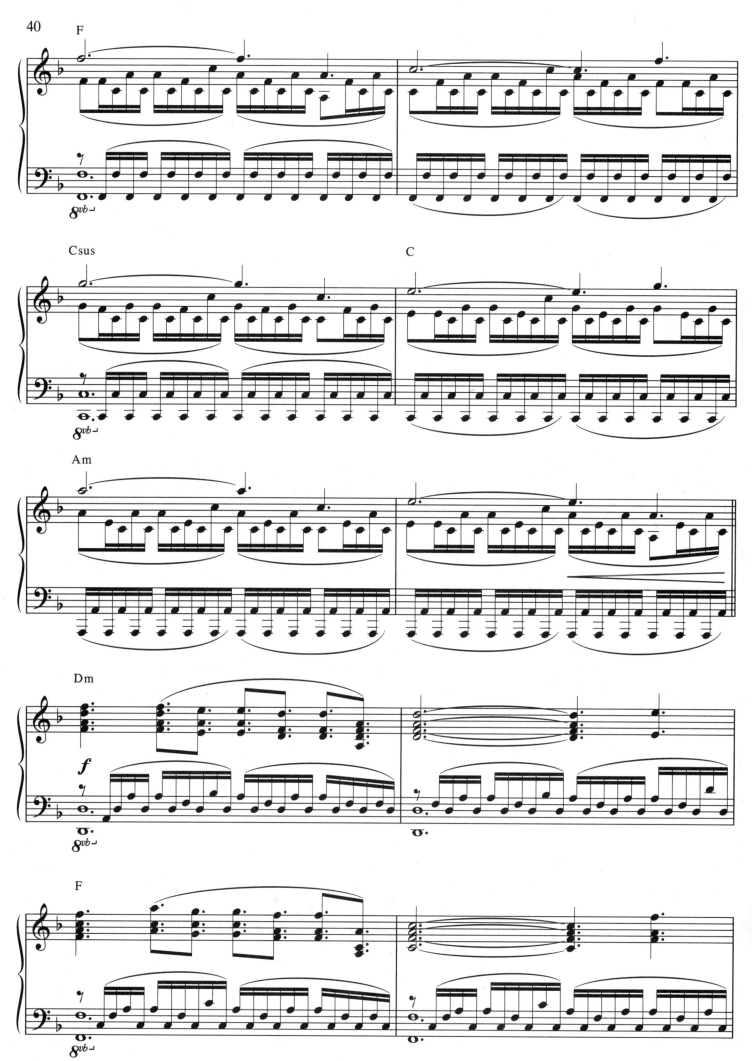

40

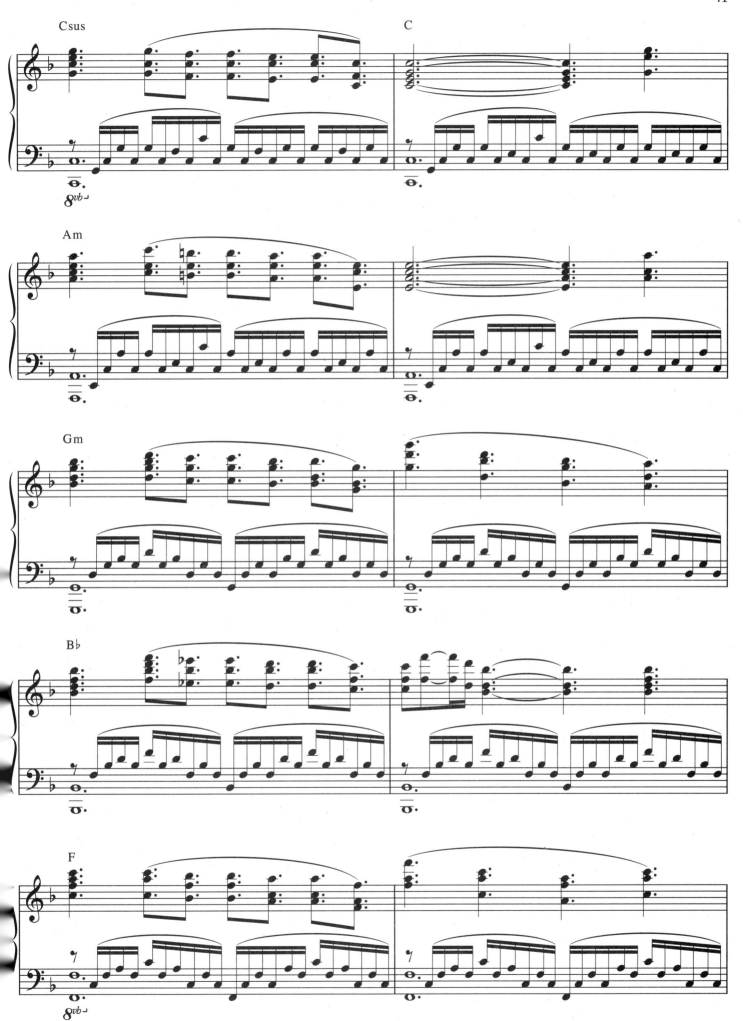

THE DARK KNIGHT OVERTURE

(from *The Dark Knight*)

Composed by
HANS ZIMMER
and JAMES NEWTON HOWARD

Mysteriously (♩ = 96)

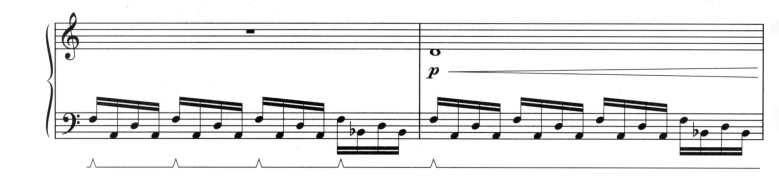

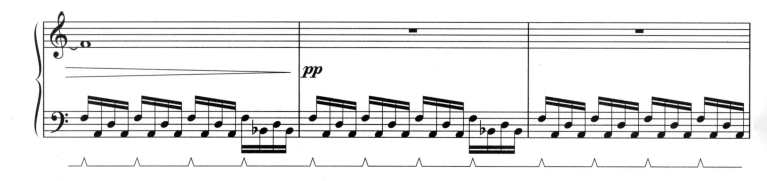

The Dark Knight Overture - 11 - 1

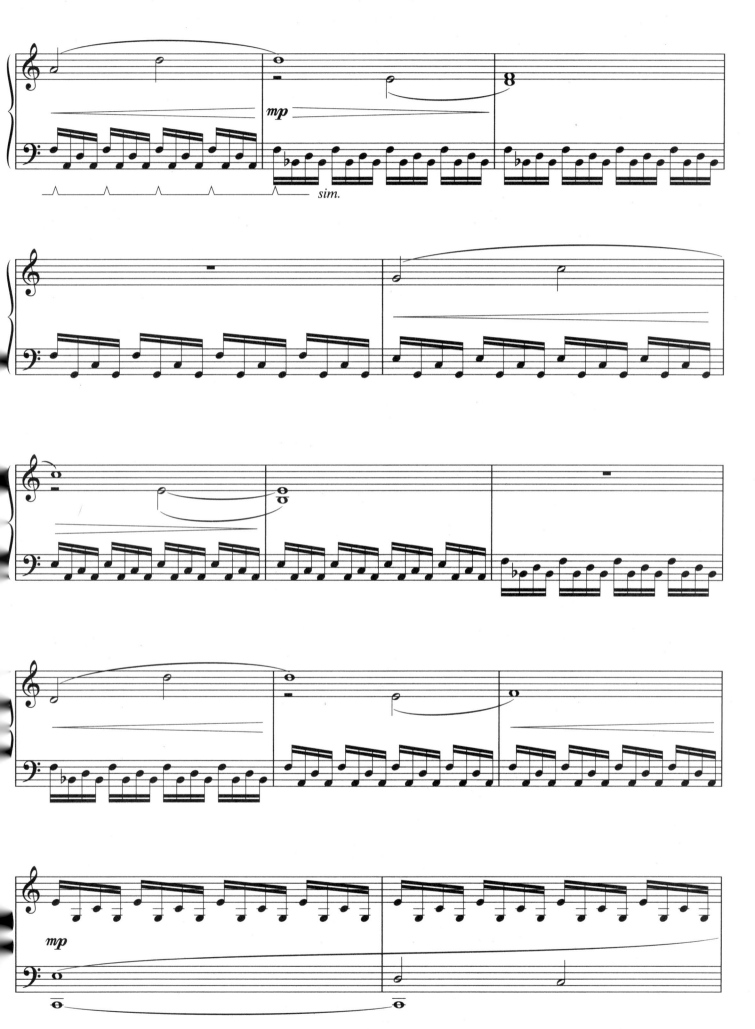

The Dark Knight Overture - 11 - 2

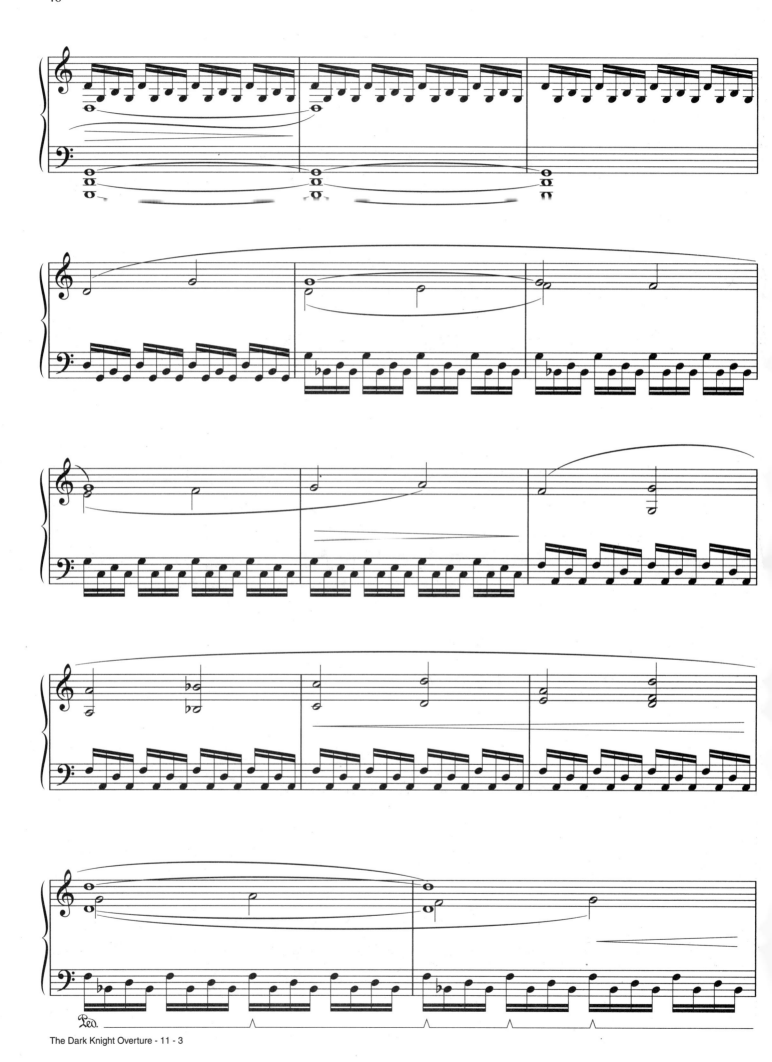

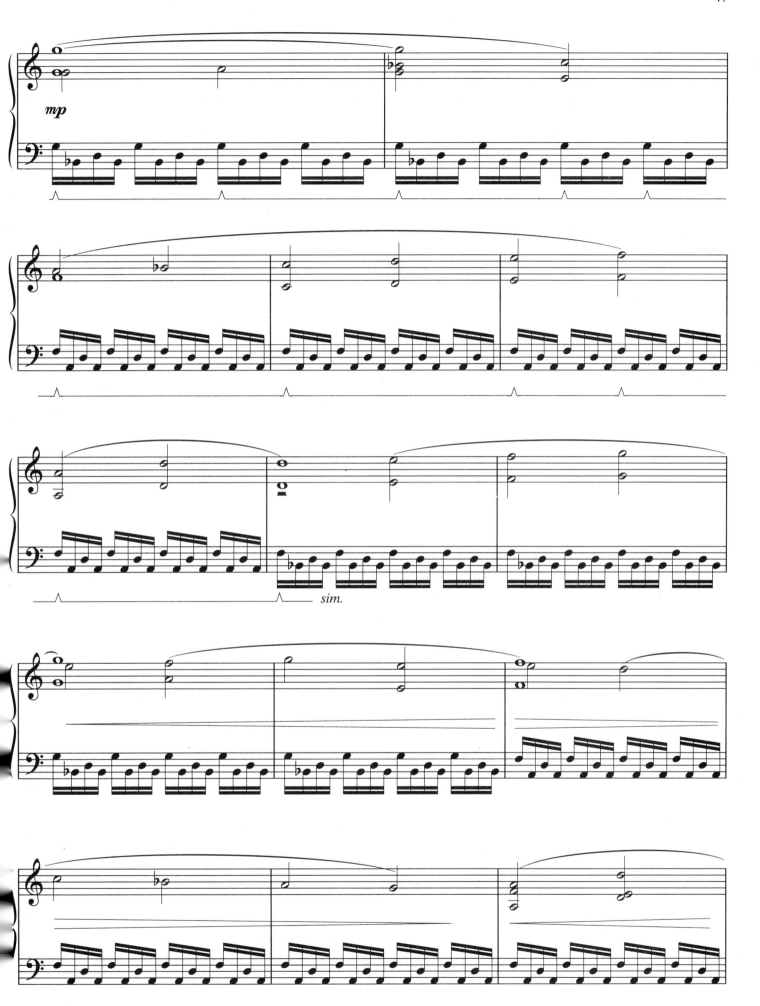

50

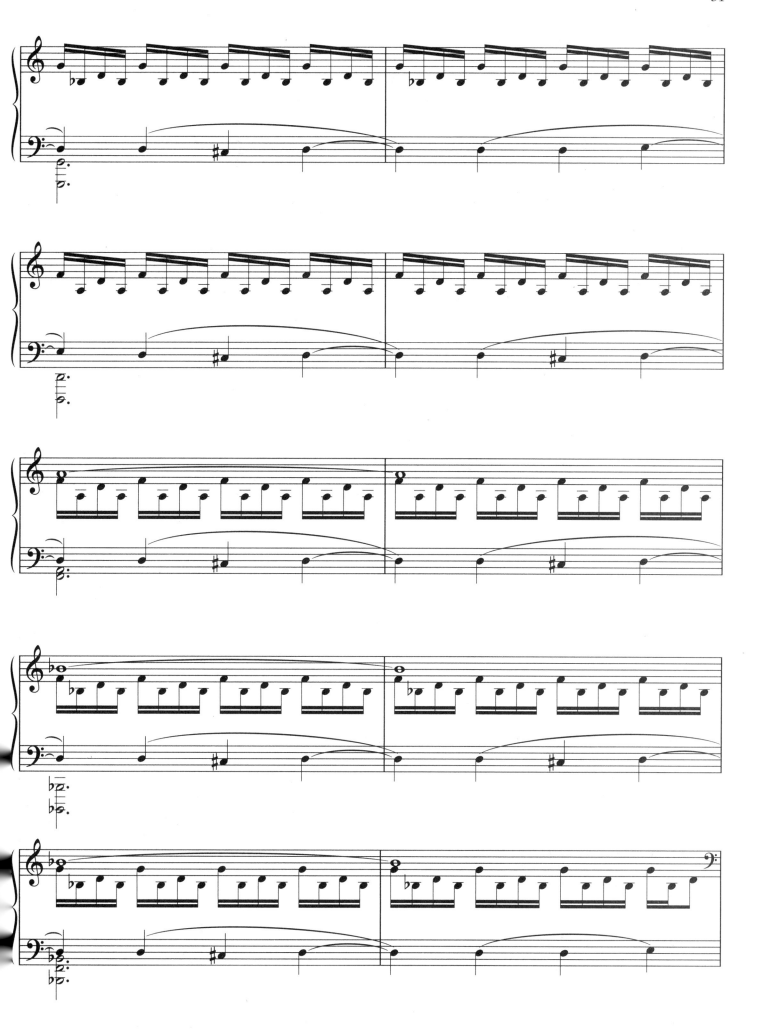

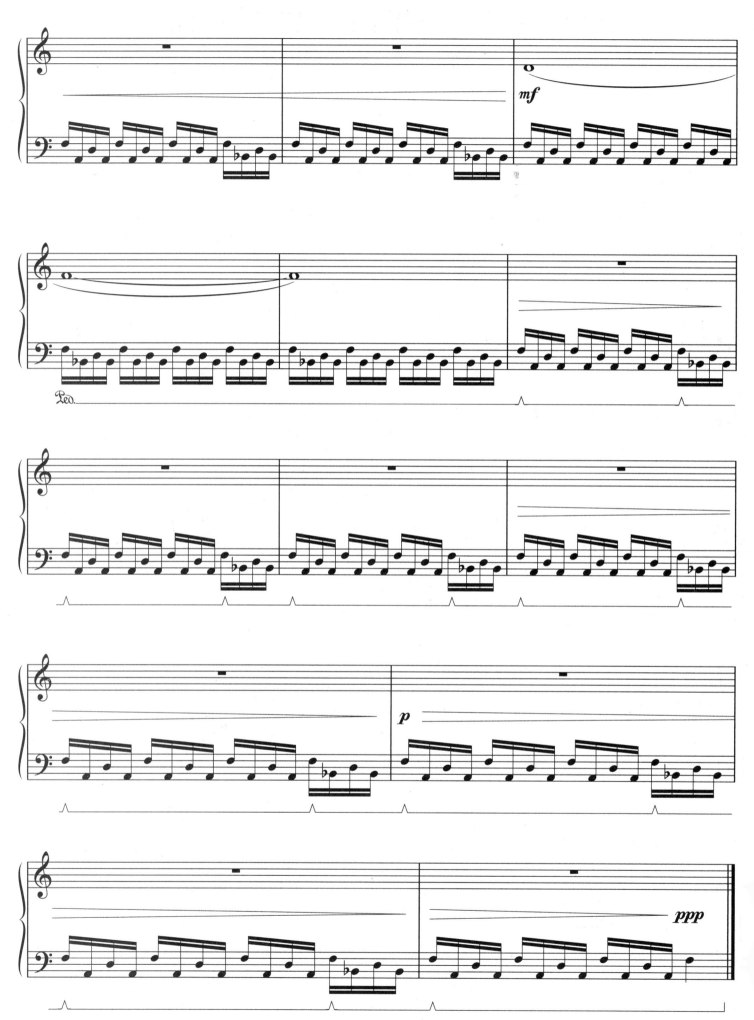

DAYS OF THUNDER (MAIN TITLE)

(from *Days of Thunder*)

Composed by
HANS ZIMMER

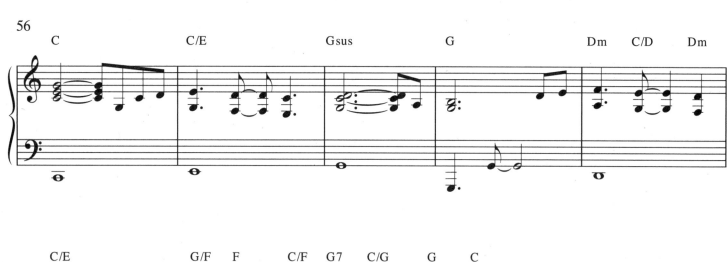

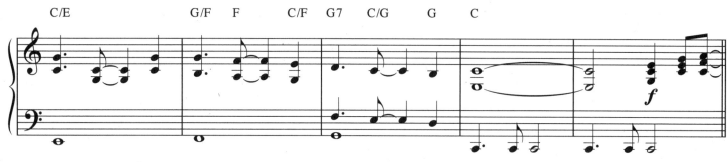

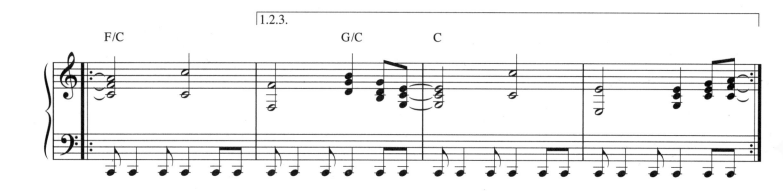

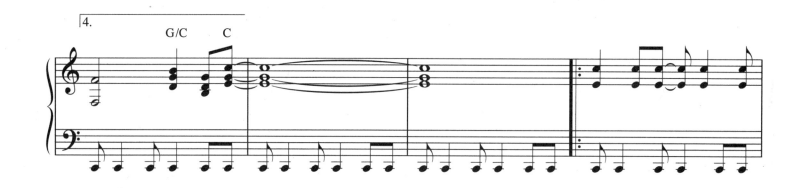

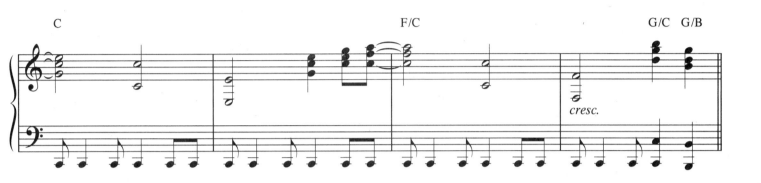

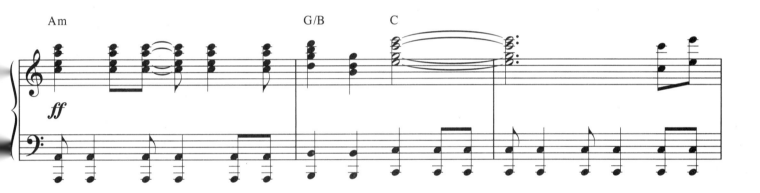

Repeat ad lib. and fade

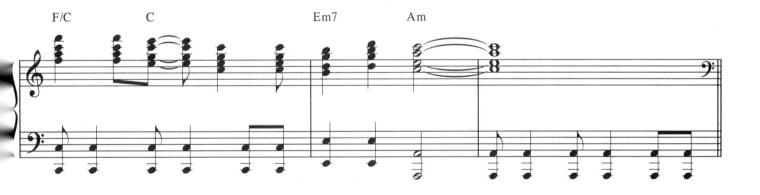

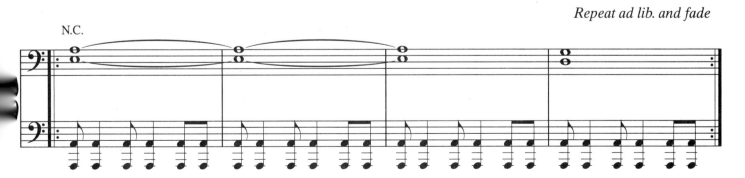

DISCOMBOBULATE

(from *Sherlock Holmes*)

Composed by
HANS ZIMMER

Slowly (♩ = 72)

Twice as fast (♩ = 142)

Discombobulate - 5 - 1

62

Discombobulate - 5 - 5

DRIVING MISS DAISY

(from *Driving Miss Daisy*)

Composed by
HANS ZIMMER

Moderately (♩ = 132)

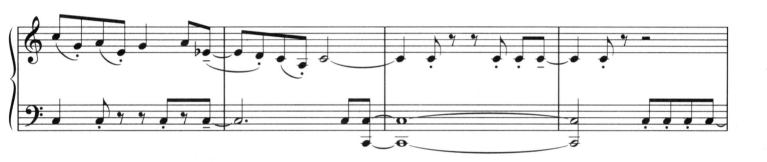

Driving Miss Daisy - 3 - 1

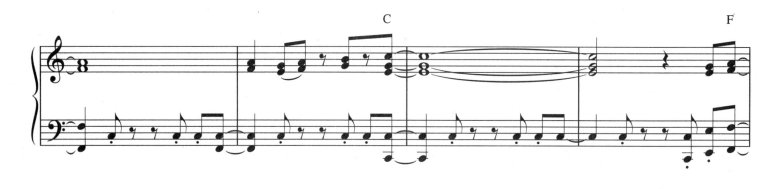

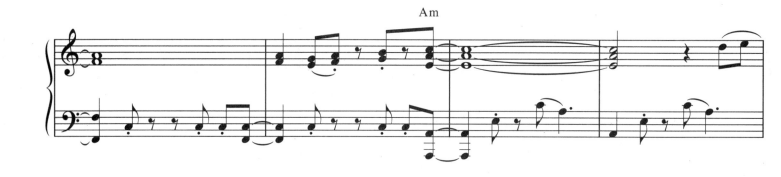

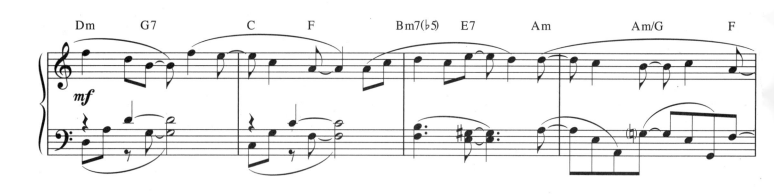

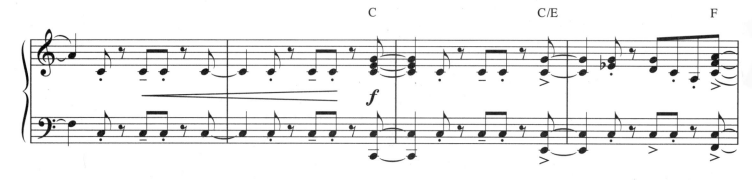

DOOMSDAY IS FAMILY TIME

(from *The Simpsons Movie*)

Composed by
HANS ZIMMER and DANNY ELFMAN

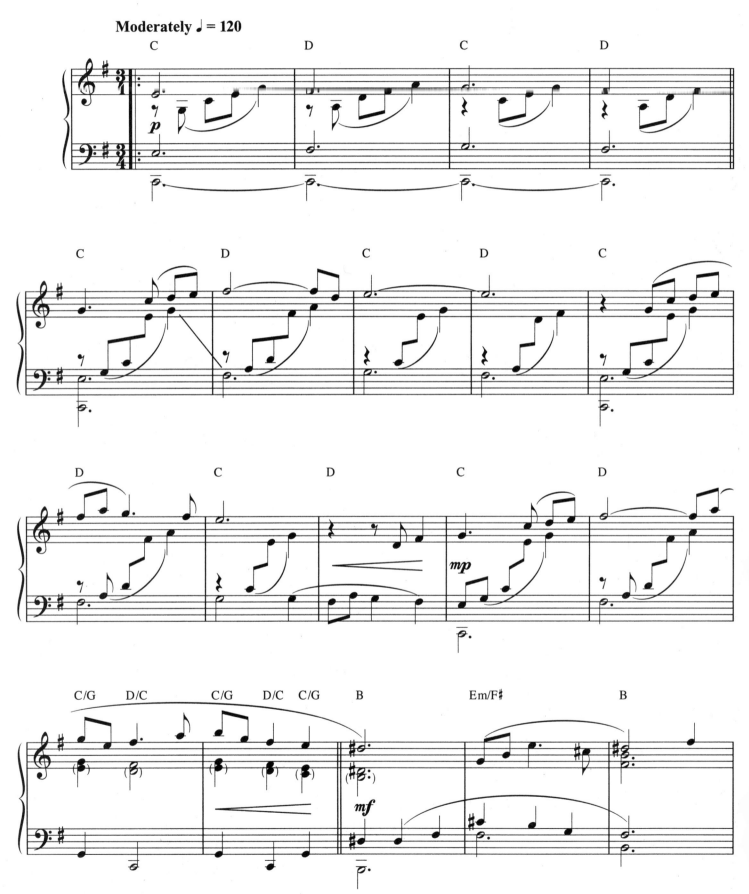

Doomsday Is Family Time - 2 - 1

DREAM IS COLLAPSING

(from *Inception*)

Composed by
HANS ZIMMER

Mysterious march (♩ = 120)

Dream Is Collapsing - 4 - 1

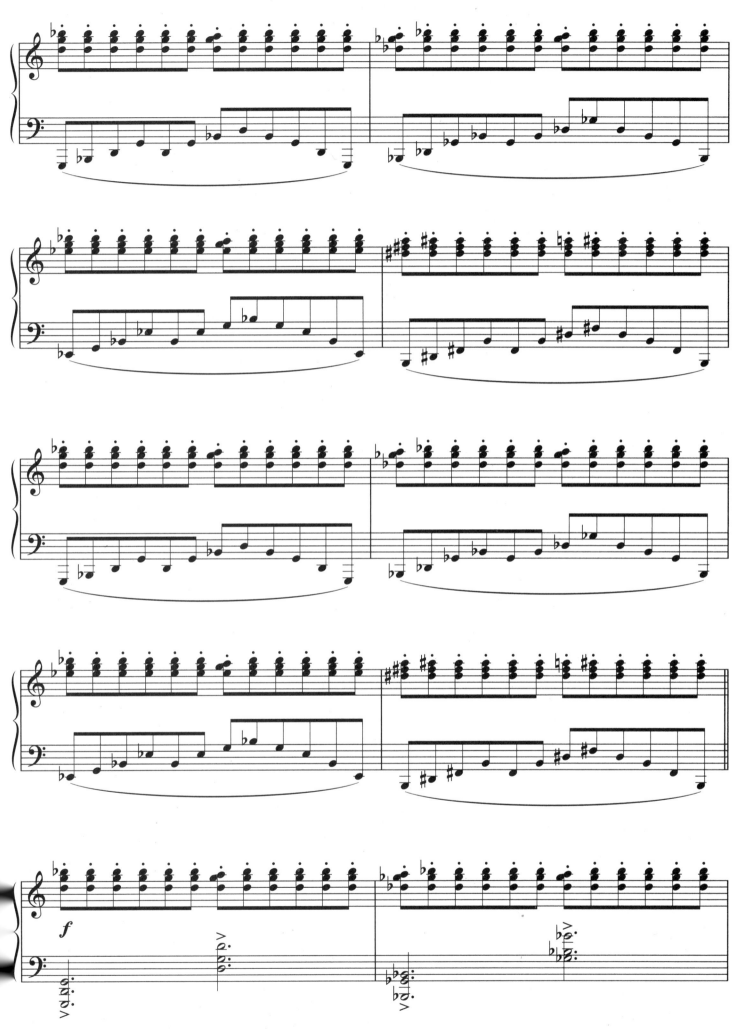

DRINK UP ME HEARTIES

(from *Pirates of the Caribbean: At World's End*)

Music by
HANS ZIMMER,
GEOFFREY ZANELLI, LORNE BALFE
and HENRY PRYCE JACKSON

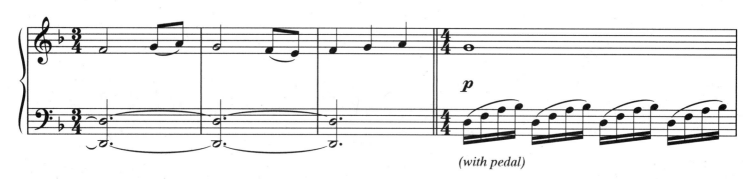

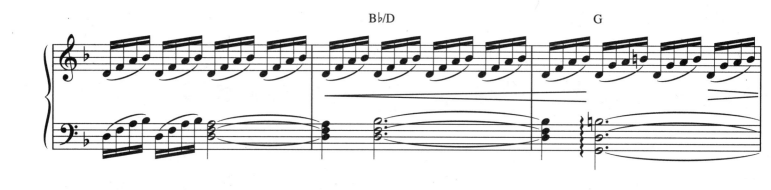

Drink Up - 10 - 1

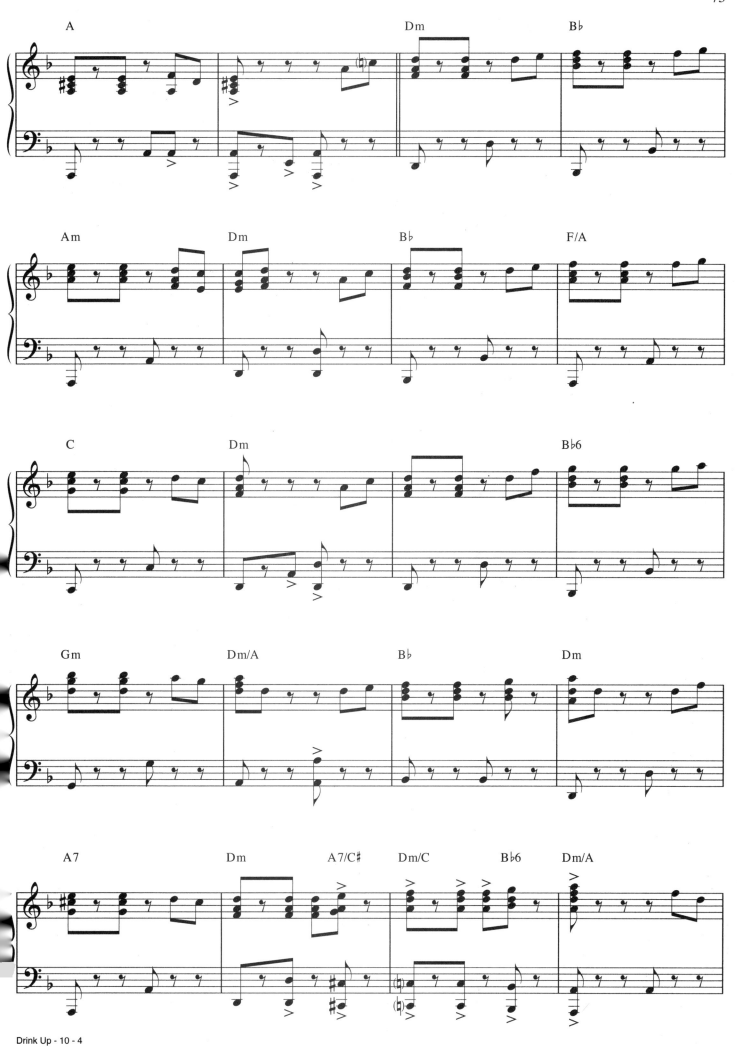

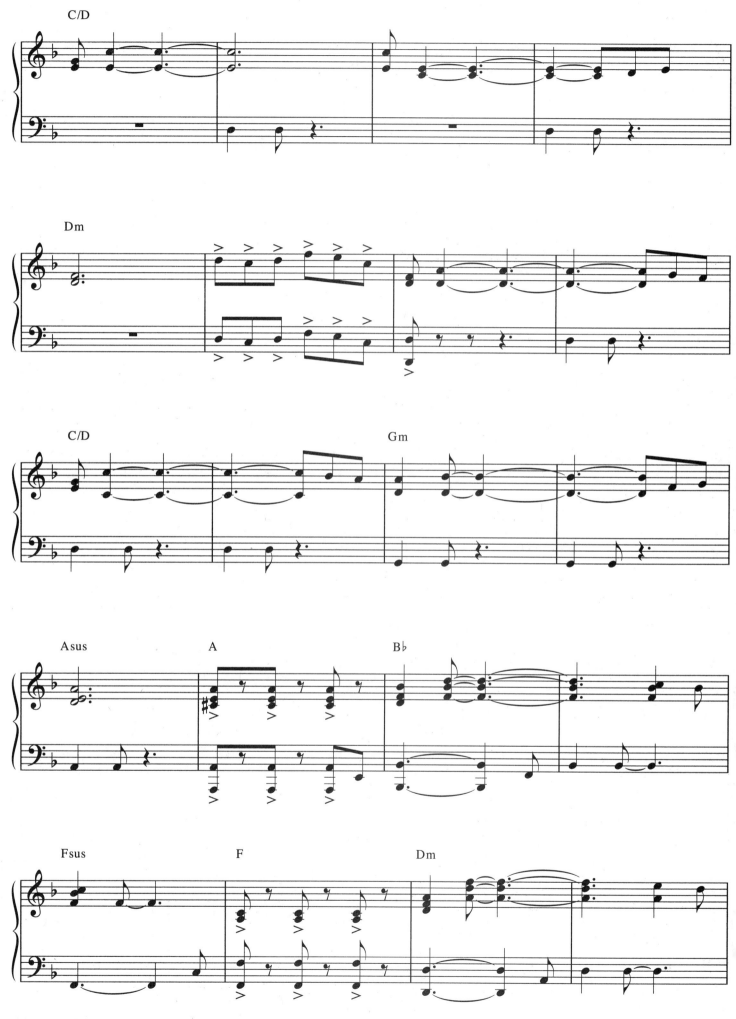

HOMELAND (Main Title)

(from *Spirit: Stallion of the Cimarron*)

Composed by
HANS ZIMMER

Moderate march, with spirit (♩ = 96)

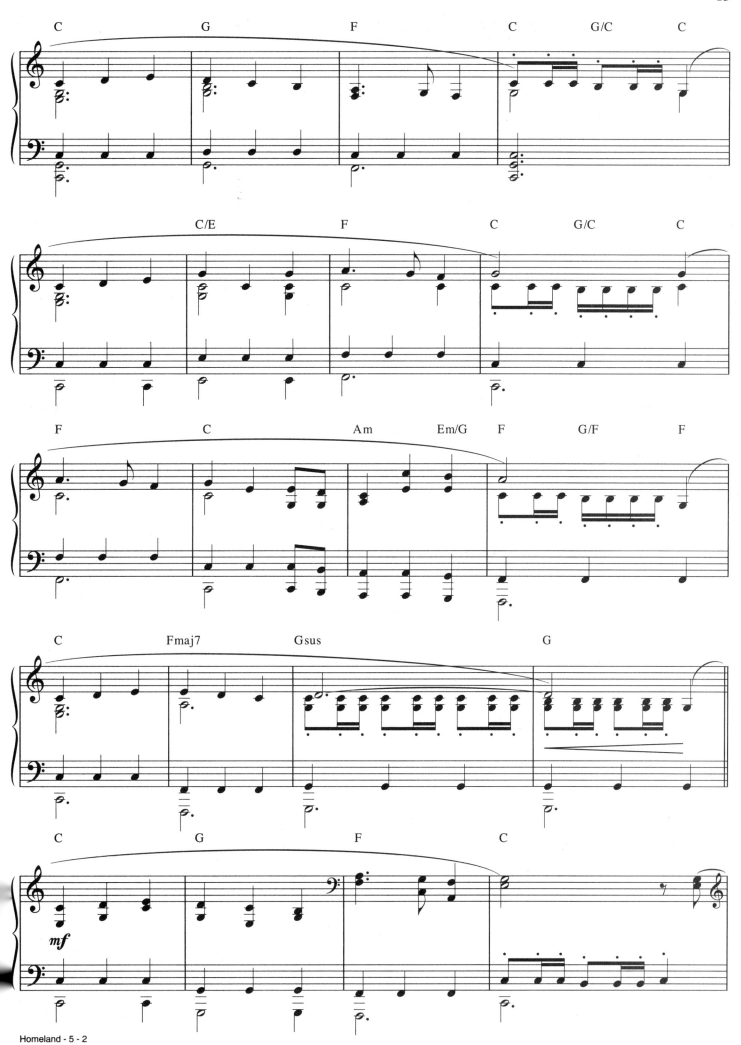

LIFE GOES ON
(from *A League of Their Own*)

Written by
HANS ZIMMER

Life Goes On - 7 - 1

HONOR HIM

(from the DreamWorks film *Gladiator*)

Composed by
HANS ZIMMER

Moderately slow (♩ = 72)

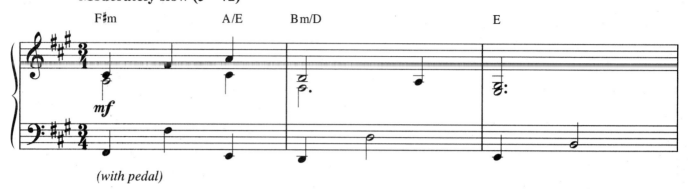

(with pedal)

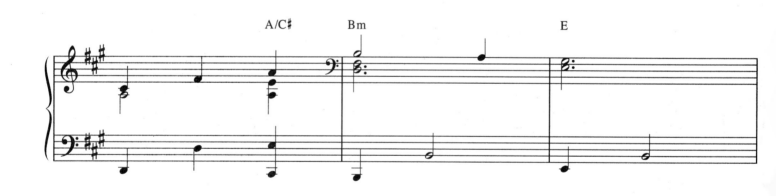

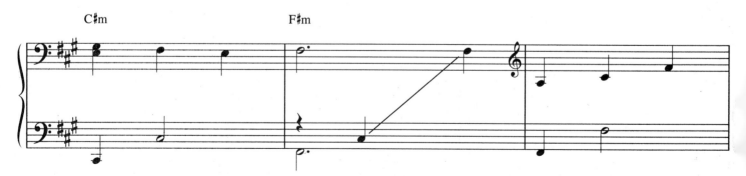

Honor Him - 2 - 1

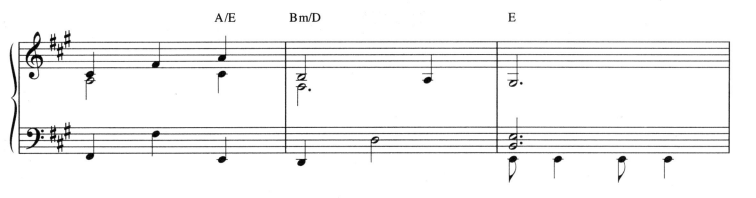

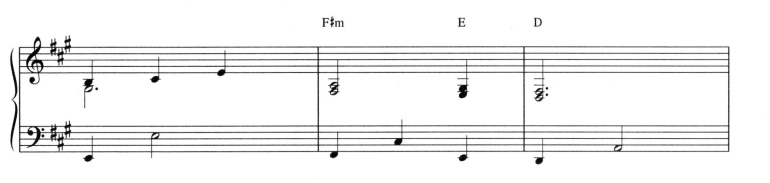

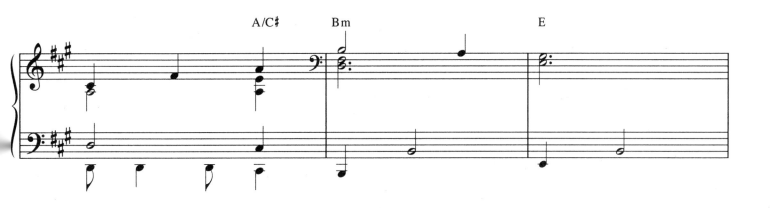

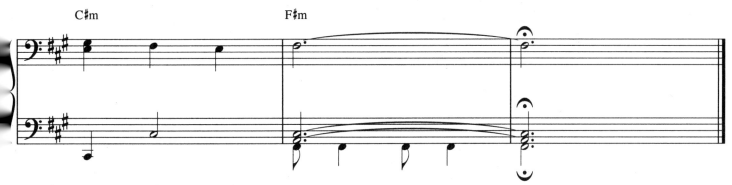

Honor Him - 2 - 2

IN THE BEGINNING

(from *The Bible*)

Composed by
HANS ZIMMER and LORNE BALFE

Majestically ♩ = (141)

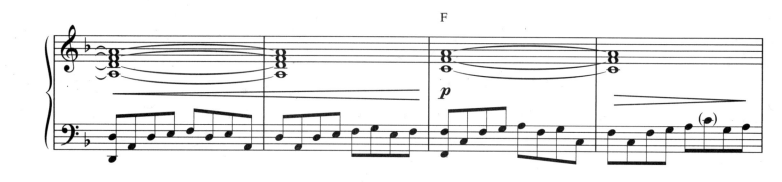

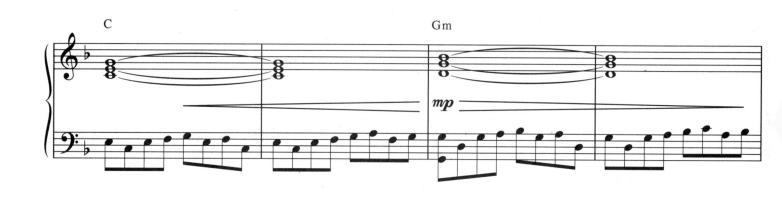

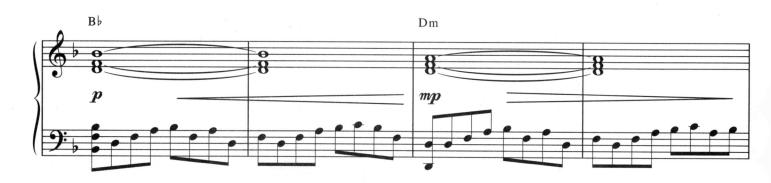

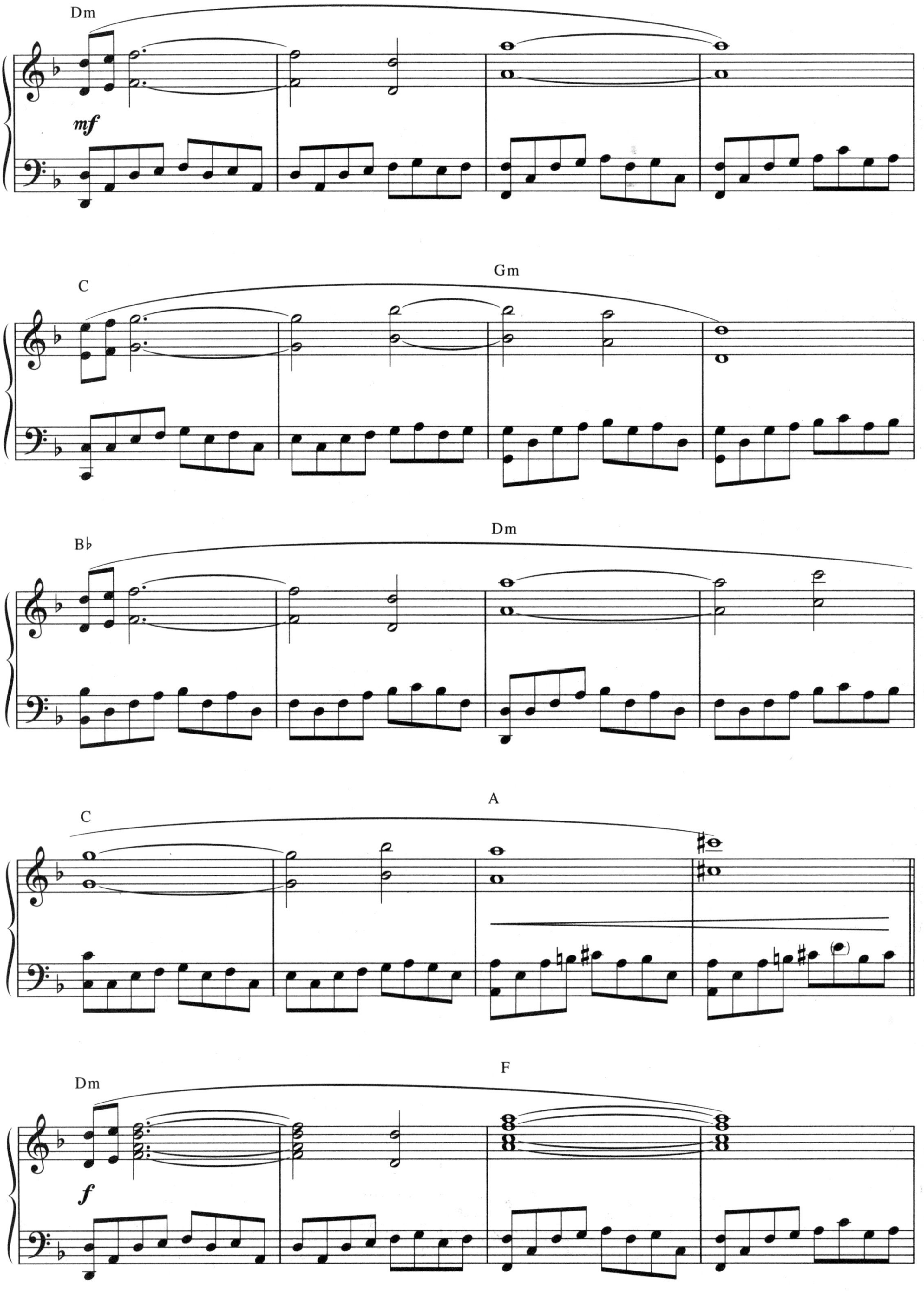
Dm
F
mf
C
Gm
B♭
Dm
C
A
Dm
F
f

IT'S SO OVERT IT'S COVERT

(From *Sherlock Holmes: A Game of Shadows*)

Composed by
HANS ZIMMER

Moderately (♩ = 120)

Still faster

KRYPTON'S LAST

(from *Man of Steel*)

Composed by
HANS ZIMMER

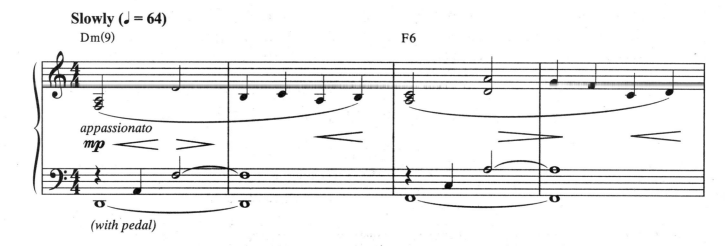

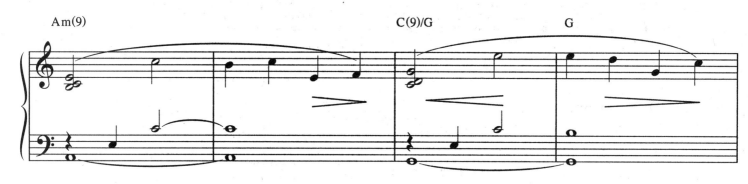

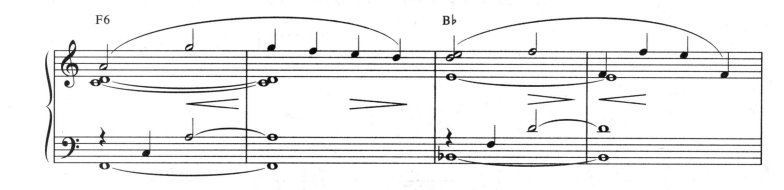

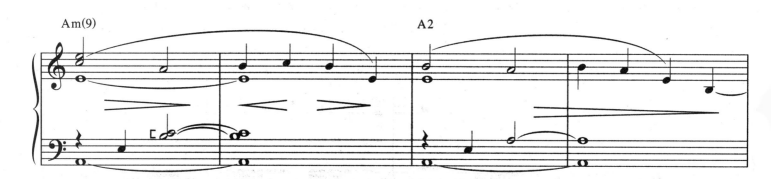

Krypton's Last - 2 - 1

MAESTRO
(from *The Holiday*)

Composed by
HANS ZIMMER

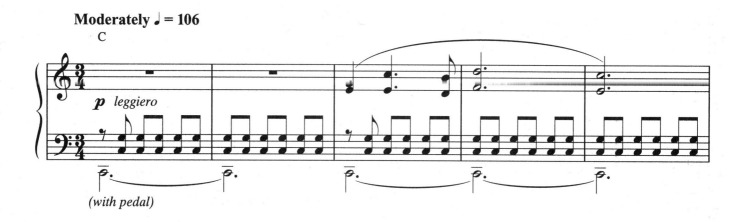

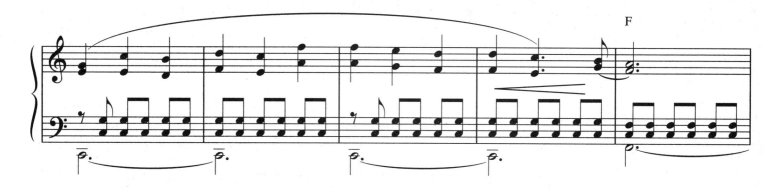

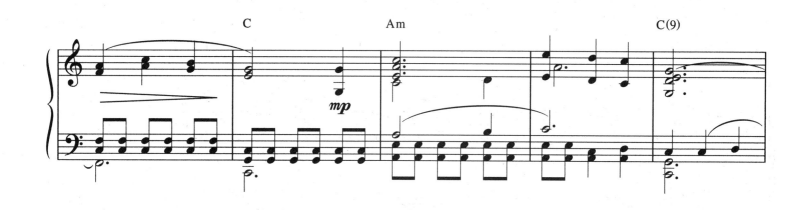

Maestro - 6 - 1

NOW WE ARE FREE

(from the DreamWorks film *Gladiator*)

Words and Music by
HANS ZIMMER,
LISA GERRARD and KLAUS BADELT

Moderately fast (♩ = 138)

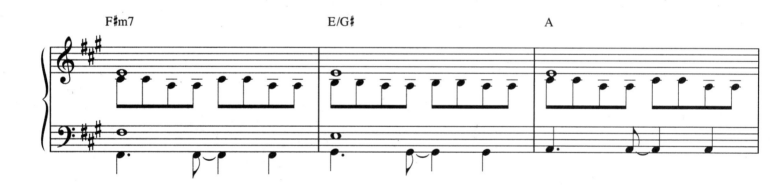

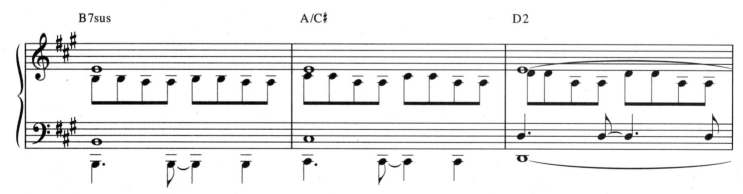

Now We Are Free - 6 - 1

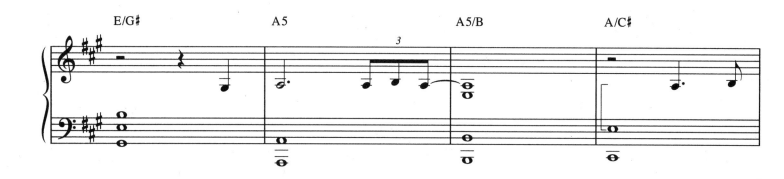

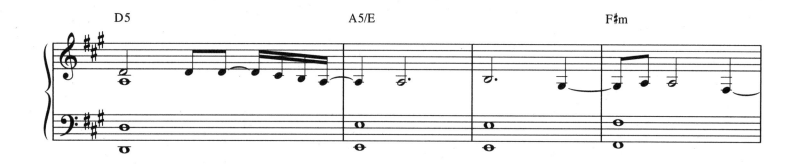

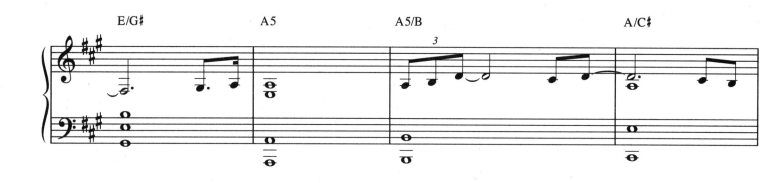

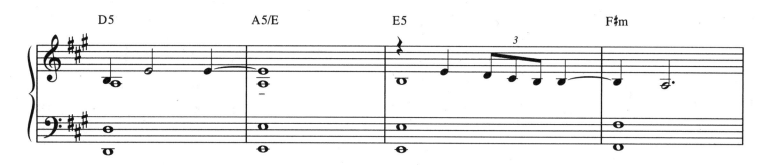

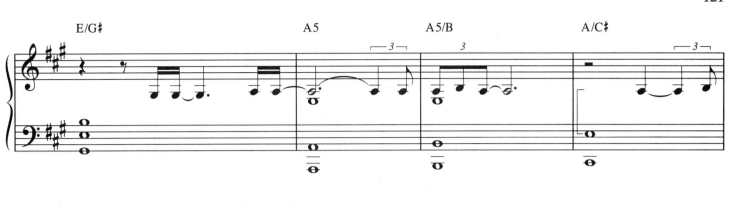

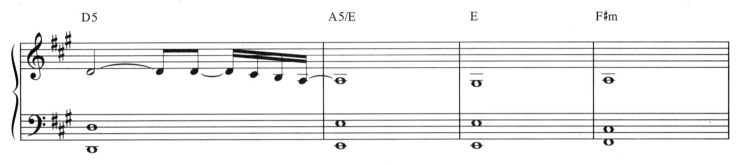

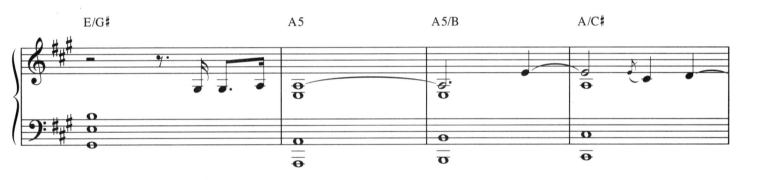

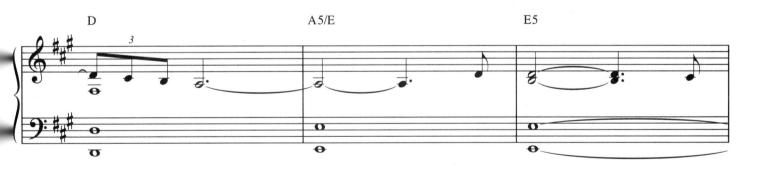

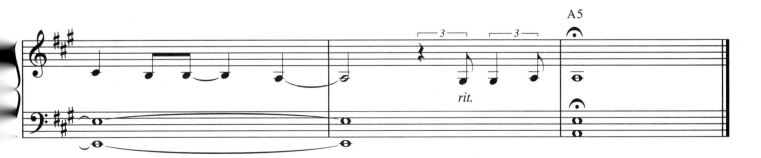

ROLL TIDE
(from *Crimson Tide*)

Composed by
HANS ZIMMER

Moderately slow ♩ = 88

126

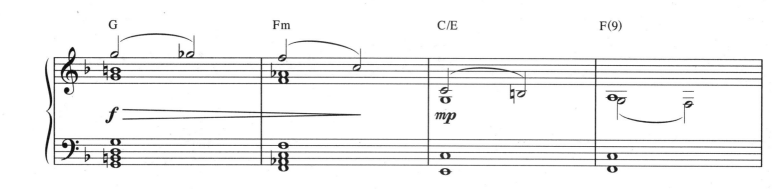

Slower ♩ = 66

E - ter - nal Fa - ther, strong to save, Whose

TENNESSEE

(from *Pearl Harbor*)

Composed by
HANS ZIMMER

Slowly, with expression (♩ = 71)

(with pedal)

Tennessee - 4 - 1

Tennessee - 4 - 2

THE NATIVITY

(from *The Bible*)

Composed by
HANS ZIMMER and LORNE BALFE

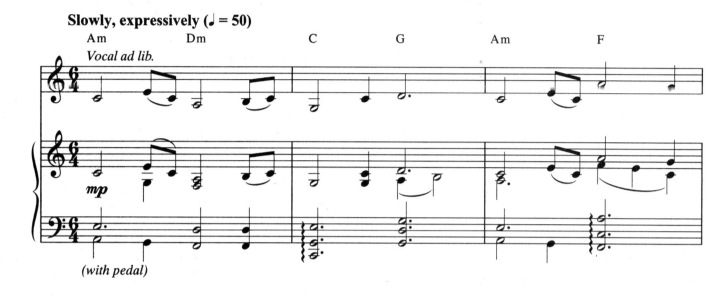

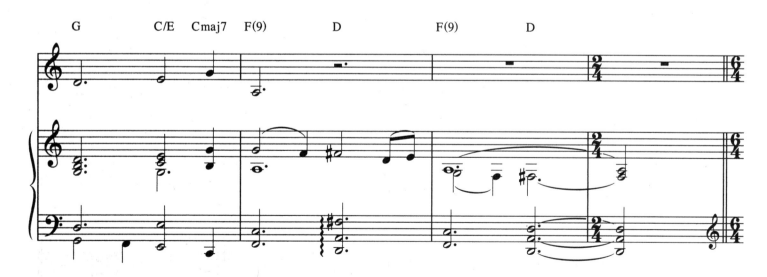

The Nativity - 3 - 1

THIS IS CLARK KENT

(from *Man of Steel*)

Composed by
HANS ZIMMER

Slowly and gently (♩ = 80)

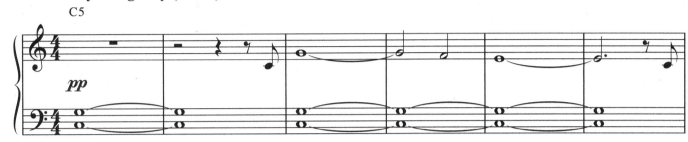

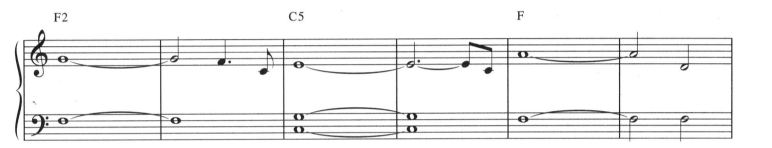

This Is Clark Kent - 3 - 1

THIS LAND

(from Walt Disney Pictures' *The Lion King*)

Music by
HANS ZIMMER and LEBO M

Slowly, with grandeur (♩ = 70)

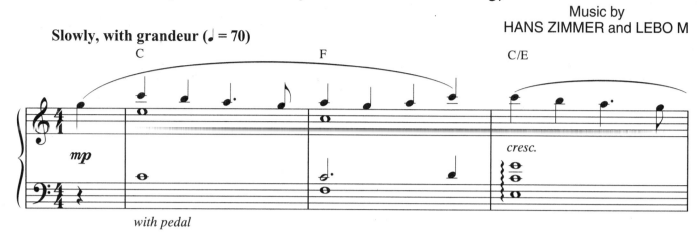

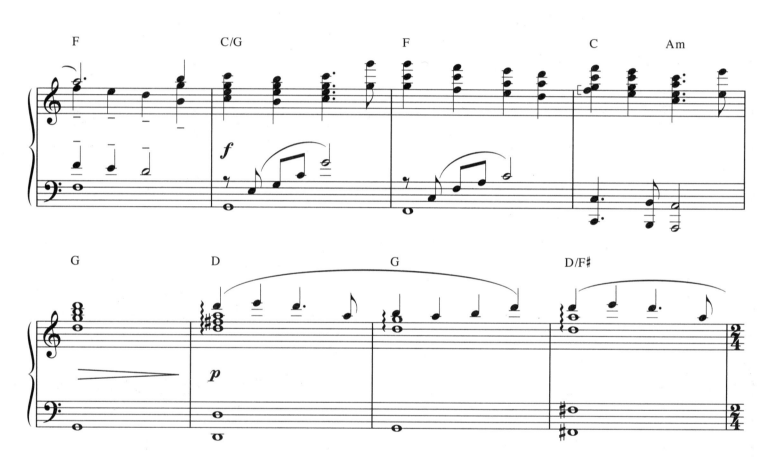

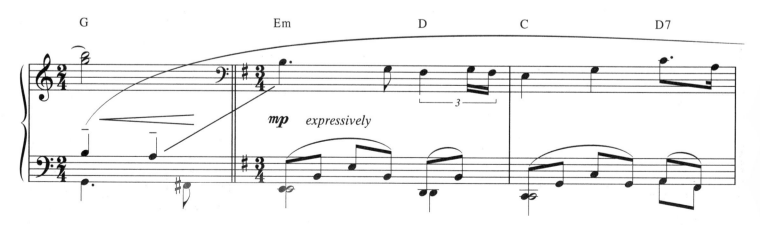

This Land - 3 - 1

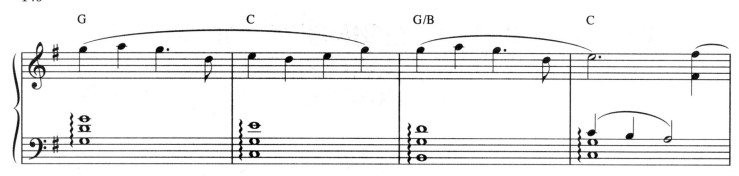

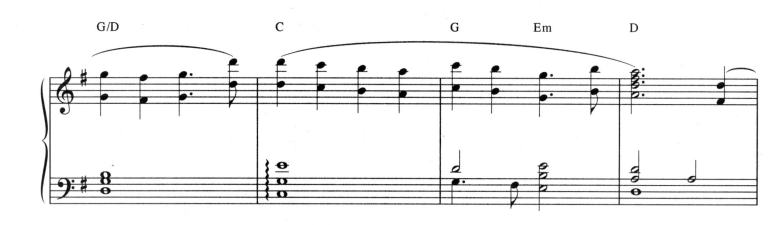

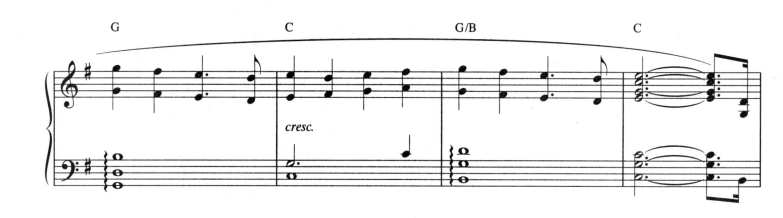

This Land - 3 - 3

WHAT ARE YOU GOING TO DO WHEN YOU ARE NOT SAVING THE WORLD

(from *Man of Steel*)

Composed by
HANS ZIMMER

Moderately slow (♩ = 80)

What Are You Going To Do
When You Are Not Saving The World - 4 - 3

144

What Are You Going To Do
When You Are Not Saving The World - 4 - 4